The Golden Year of Fan Cheng-ta

范成大

四時田園雜興六十首

THE GOLDEN YEAR OF
FAN CHENG-TA

A Chinese Rural Sequence
rendered into English verse by

GERALD BULLETT

with notes
and calligraphic decorations by

TSUI CHI

CAMBRIDGE

At the University Press

1946

CAMBRIDGE UNIVERSITY PRESS
Cambridge, New York, Melbourne, Madrid, Cape Town,
Singapore, São Paulo, Delhi, Tokyo, Mexico City

Cambridge University Press
The Edinburgh Building, Cambridge CB2 8RU, UK

Published in the United States of America by
Cambridge University Press, New York

www.cambridge.org
Information on this title: www.cambridge.org/9781107679238

First published 1946
Reprinted 1946
First paperback edition 2011

A catalogue record for this publication is available from the British Library

ISBN 978-1-107-67923-8 Paperback

CONTENTS

PREFACE

FAN CHENG-TA, author of the sequence of poems here
for the first time offered in an English rendering, lived and
died in our twelfth century, that is, during the middle years
of the Sung Dynasty. Like so many other Chinese poets, he
spent much of his life in the state service, having in A.D. 1154
passed the highest literary examination and become thereby
an 'advanced scholar'. He was born in 1126 and died in 1193,
and he is believed to have written these particular poems
during his sixtieth year, a year of rural retirement from official
life because of failing health. His talents were both military
and diplomatic. By firmness and shrewd strategy he succeeded
in quelling border rebellions, during his term of office as
military governor of Ssuchuan; and in an earlier year he had
greatly distinguished himself in a diplomatic mission to the
court of a victorious ex-enemy, the Prince of the Golden Race.
As governor he made a point of collecting poets round him
and using them on his staff. 'He employed them to the best
advantage', remarks a Chinese historian, 'overlooking their
small faults'. One of these, Yang Wan-li, has left a tribute
both personal and literary: 'He surpasses all other contem-
porary poets. Myself, need I be too modest about my own
poetry? But to him I bow my head. In conversation, whether
on the newest and most curious subjects or on the highest
philosophical abstractions, he was no less a master than were
the scholars of the Tsin-Sung period. As for his poems, when

the work is weighty it has the force of a river in flood, and when it is in miniature form it has the delicate modelling of an ear of corn, rich without excess, precise without tenuity.' We are told, further, that Governor Fan's administration in Ssuchuan was exceptionally wise, benevolent, and fruitful of good to all classes of the people, from the peasants, whom he cared for in times of difficulty, to the army, whose generals he chose with great shrewdness (for their poetical talent, one hopes) and whose equipment he studied to improve; and that whenever he wrote a poem, in the abundant leisure he enjoyed after masterfully solving these official problems, no sooner was the ink dry upon the paper than 'tens of thousands of men and women were copying and reading it. Calligraphers would write it on silk screens or on fans, and give them to their friends.' One is hardly surprised to learn that no previous governor of Ssuchuan had been so honoured.

My part in the present undertaking is dedicated, without his permission, to a distinguished historian of Chinese civilization, my friend Mr Tsui Chi, who with untiring kindness opened for me the eight-and-twenty doors into each of the sixty poems here translated. Read as a continuing sequence they present a poet's picture of rural life in the district of Soochow eight centuries ago. Each in the original consists of four, end-stopped, seven-word lines, rhymed *a a b a* or *a b c b*. Classical Chinese being an extremely allusive and an extremely condensed language, and the peculiar music of Chinese poetry being strictly inimitable in English, a translator into English verse has no alternative but to find a form of his own. When Tsui Chi had supplied me with literal equivalents (where they could be found) of the twenty-eight words in each poem, I found that for me the best plan was to render each long Chinese line in two not so long English ones; and taking a middle way between formalism and freedom I have used half-rhyme, and other coupling devices, as well as full rhyme. My immersion in the mind of a twelfth-century Chinese poet during the midsummer weeks of this year has been a rich experience, of which some part, I hope, may be shared with the reader of the following pages.

G. B.

AUTUMN 1945

Early Spring

柳花深巷午雞聲

1

But for the cockerel calling the noon hour,
No voice is heard in the lane of willow-flower.
The young leaves of the mulberry, half-uncurl'd,
Are showing their green tips to the warm world.
Waking from quiet dreams, where I drowse in my chair,
With nothing to do but enjoy the bright air,
I look from my window, flooded now with noon,
And see the silkworm break from her cocoon.

2

Under the silver lash of the small rain,
The quicken'd earth is bringing forth again:
Ten thousand spears of grass and sudden flowers
Spring up to meet the showers.
Behind the house the unweeded small demesne
Shows a patchwork pattern of varying green,
And from the neighbouring garden bamboo-roots
Creeping under the wall send up new shoots.

3

In the high fields the green of the wheat runs
To join the mountain curve, green and bronze.
The river meadows, not yet under plow,
A darker, more luxuriant, greenness show.
The village, aglow with flowering almond and peach,
Looks like a picture drawn with silver stitch:
And there the people, with song, dancing, and drum,
Make festival because the spring is come.

4

Now to the field-shrine, from home and hearth
We bring our offerings to the spirits of earth,
Faggots and rushes, a dedicated hoard,
And food in an ancient vessel newly prepared.
Whatever, O Priestess, the lifted lid disclose,
Don't wrinkle, Reverend One, your aged nose:
Though you find the food insipid it's not so thin
As the ritual wine you'll get at the village inn.

5

After the festival of the burning of cash,
The drums a diminishing thunder, the paper ash,
At sundown the old man, having taken a drop,
Goes zigzag homewards, on a friendly prop.
Strewn on the grass, flowers and leafy boughs
Lie listless, as the serene air allows:
And he recalls, seeing the disarray,
That children have been here at play.

6

Trumpeted rumour of horsemen from the east
Fills every lane and field with clamour of feast.
The villagers swarm and stare,
Agog to see the galloping hosts appear.
And when, like a bright cloud, on noiseless hooves
Into one's far vision the procession moves—
Look, neighbour, to your cow! She's in the way.
Tie her west of the gate, where she can't stray.

7

Now is the salad festival of spring,
When girls go revelling.
With flowers fresh, this morning of the year,
They skirt their limbs and cover their dark hair.
Flower-laden, under a clear sky,
The boats go by,
Either Ling Yen being the end in view,
Or the wide panorama of Hu Chiu.

8

After the ritual sweeping of the tomb
The families from the city turn for home,
Having for tribute given the untasted jar
Of green-plum wine to the dead ancestor.
Long is the day and the road beautiful
That leads at last to the gate of the old wall.
Here in this arbour, under a friendly thatch,
We warm the wine and set a cup for each.

9

The rain over, I put my sandals on,
To walk where earlier wayfarers have gone,
Whose horses' hooves, imprinting in the mud
These brimming winecups, mark their joyous road.
My dog, following at heel as he's bid,
Soon forgets his master and runs ahead,
Till reaching a broad brook he stands at check,
Then soberly, unbidden, ambles back.

10

Swink how we may, evenings or early morn,
Our garden crops bring only a bare return.
The seeds once planted, set in careful rows,
Children and birds must be accounted foes.
Here is a needling thorn-hedge, finger-high;
Here young bamboos shoot up to greet the sky.
Let's now, to trick these thieving friends of ours,
Turn fishermen and net the cherry-flowers.

11

Today, with lifting heart and bow'd back,
Of rice-seed we open the first sack.
The thunderquake, which puts an end to drouth
And draws a blind over the crested south,
Is filling the fields with water, drop by drop,
And all the signs foretell a decent crop.
See, there, how the wallowing tide
Slaps at the bridge's underside.

[14]

Under his mulberry tree the goodman grows
Spring vegetables in nicely measured rows,
Mustard, and chives, and cabbage green and lush,
Which in due season at the brook he'll wash,
And singling out the choicest specimens
Will carry them to market. There he spends
On salt and wine the money newly won,
And with them gets him home at set of sun.

Late Spring

柴青蓴菜卷荷香

13

Close-folding lettuce, lotus-scented, green
With the satin bloom of faggots' lichen-stain,
Spring onions white as snow and smooth as jade,
And celery trimm'd with many a sprouting bud:
Of these good things, a pilgrim under sail,
I gather abundance for an evening meal,
And under my awning, here on Heng Tang,
Shelter from wind and rain the night long.

14

On the shores of a desolate region of lake and sky,
The new-dug ivory roots of lotus lie.
Green coins of water-lily, lying so still,
Persuade us half to forget the gradual swell.
Now is the plum season, gusty and quick,
With petals flying and fruit soon to pick.
Savouring the hour I mark where bulrush shoots
Come sidling up from long lateral roots.

15

Butterflies, sauntering lazily here and there,
Enter the vegetable flowers pair by pair.
I bathe in the golden stream of the long day,
Having in mind no guest will come my way.
But hark! A bark! And from over the bamboo fence
There's a sudden scatter of silly fugitive hens!
I spend no time wondering who it can be:
A merchant come to buy my leaves of tea.

16

At the flood's edge, among green duckweeds plashing,
The islet-dweller is doing her household washing.
On this day of Shang Ch'ih a man must roam,
Though chilly air may bid him stay at home.
Twilight is falling. Frogs, the night long,
Keep up their harsh, sonorous, croaking song:
Fair omen that in this fine year of rain
Our rice will yield ten portions of good grain.

17

Garden trees, in the cool glow of dawn,
Put on new green to enjoy the new sun.
Breakfasting early I walk in paradise
And watch my boys transplant the seedling rice.
Ten thousand falling petals scatter my path:
Mulberry and hemp show yet but meagre growth.
At every sauntering turn a wanderer meets
Odour of spices borne on a light breeze.

18

For thirty days, jealous of visitors,
The silkworm lives unseen, behind shut doors.
Even the nearest of neighbours will refrain
From making footprints in the dusty lane.
Only on golden mornings, when the breeze
Scarce stirs the dew that lingers in the trees,
They come together to gather the mulberry leaf,
With serious smile and conversation brief.

19

Today his plat of cultivated mud
Becomes an island sinking in the flood.
Today, from his snail-shell cottage, every year,
He sees the tidemark creeping up his door.
Did he not know by hard experience
The weakness of a planted water-fence,
Time and again he would have plied his oar
In search of rushes to defend the shore.

20

Here downy, pointed reedlings, scabbard-bound,
In fragrant bundles wrap each other round.
Here russet berries somewhat wanly gleam,
Nature not having finished painting them.
Nevertheless, remembering my daughters and sons,
I find on the way plenty of likely ones;
And the children greet me gaily, seeing my pick
In the bamboo cage, at the end of my walking stick.

21

This day of the rice-in-husk festival,
The rain is silken, and perpetual.
The wax from my open'd bottle floats away;
I warm the wine and enjoy its fresh bouquet.
Peony blossoms from the calyx drop;
Already the cherry-tree carries a glowing crop.
These flying silks, these petals on the wing,
Cannot subdue today the spirit of spring.

22

After the rains, morning, airy and good,
Finds some of the country folk still in bed.
Here, the high window fills with dawn,
Of soft radiance, of dazzling sun.
This old one, roused by rustle and chirping calls,
Lies listening to the golden orioles.
The house boy, already up and about,
Opens the door to let a swallow out.

23

And now, rivers rising and seas full,
Our world is water, with scarcely an interval.
Going in search of seasonable fish,
Soon we return with all that we could wish.
The sea-pig comes upstream; the edible
Miscanthus shoots are now ready to pull;
The oriental lilac blooms anew;
And the fish called Yellow Flower swims into view.

24

Few come this way, and if a stranger should,
See how the birds dart off, into the wood!
Shadows of dove-grey dusk the hills obscure,
And gathering reach my faggot-builded door.
In a boat light as a leaf, still visible,
My lad-of-all-work plies his single scull.
Alone, I weave my fence, of lithe bamboo,
And ducks go primly homewards, two by two.

Summer

梅子金黄杏子肥

25

Heavy the trees with load of golden plum,
To mellow age the almond fruit is come,
Flowers of the rape-turnip bloom and blow,
And the long barley blossoms into snow.
Long and serene my solitary day
Hedged in with summer, and never a passer-by,
Except these bright-wing'd insect-travellers
Going about their glittering affairs.

26

Soochow, in this fifth moon of the year,
Is cool as the cornfields come into ear.
Though padded their clothes with cotton stuff
The rice-field workers are scarcely warm enough.
Around the seedling roots, in a black swarm,
Innumerable tadpoles swim and squirm;
For the spring rains, in these fields of the rice crop,
Have covered the ground with water a foot deep.

27

Two seasons' crops have yielded us so much,
A peck of corn brings only a hundred cash.
Even the peasant-farmers, many and poor,
Enjoy abundance this surprising year.
The oven's crammed with baking, and we know
Our cooking-pots assured their modest due,
Till the golden western wind shall blow again,
To bring the season of ripening rice-grain.

28

Cocoons, in boiling vats put to proof,
Thicken the rising water with snow-white surf.
The wheels of the spinning-cart buzz: the spray falls
Pat on the workers' dried-leaf overalls.
These mulberry-girls cross hands, as for a game,
To give each other joy of the great time,
Pleased that the coarser silk has proved to be rare
And the fine filament plentiful this year.

29

Day after day the married daughters come,
To labour at the loom.
And year by year, swifter than dragonflies,
The tax-collectors swoop upon the prize.
This year, however, the mulberry and the worm
Have thrived together on even the smallest farm,
And the women are content with the yellow leavings
Allowed to them for their own weavings.

30

From the low fields the water is forced up
To run with the river, and thence again to the top
To keep those watercourses flowing full
Which irrigate the highest fields of all.
These dispensations are the work of man,
No part of Nature's plan:
Upon this water-engine, age after age,
The feet of the young men tread with punctual pace.

31

Sons in the fields all day, daughters at evening
Spinning hemp and weaving,
These with nimble fingers and strong arms
Contrive to keep things going on our farms.
This little grandchild, five years short of twelve,
As yet can neither spin nor deeply delve:
Yet even he, even so,
Under the mulberry his melon-seeds would grow.

32

Mulberry, sophora, fair-grown and beautiful,
Hold themselves still, in air serenely cool.
The rhamnus grows in pairs, his leaves curl'd
Like rats' ears, his colour emerald.
Only the Three Dukes, the saying goes,
May look at the Three Trees.
Yet here, at his northern window, unafraid,
A simple man enjoys their benign shade.

33

Bedew'd with sweat and grimed with golden dust,
He lingers by the garden, an unknown guest,
Breaking a long journey to slake his drouth
With water from the well's fragrant mouth.
I lend my gate for him to lean upon,
And here's a millstone where he sits him down.
A freshet of wind in the willow-shaded air
With cooling touch tempers the noon hour.

34

In a many-acre field of lotus-flowers
I drift my boat and let loose my oars.
The way is hidden amid a mass of bloom,
And evening finds me still forgetful of home.
They who await me there know full well
My whereabouts, though seeing not my sail,
Whence, every now and again, into their sight,
Small waterfowls rise up, in sudden flight.

35

Time was he worked like others with plow and hoe,
But now a-gathering caltrops he must go:
Blood from his prickt fingers, trickling down,
Tinges the pale water vermilion.
Field who has none, nor any means to buy,
Must plant and reap in water, where he may:
And even then he can't hope to escape,
In these hard times, the tax-collectors' rape.

36

Shadows extend, under the slanting sun:
The cicadas' bubbling noise goes on and on.
The night falls, but frogs, too wide awake,
Cannot forbear their automatic croak.
Use now the art of being dull of sense,
And so by feigning find indifference:
How else may the dream-soul, each mortal has,
On viewless wing approach my bed of grass?

Autumn

杷菊垂珠滴露紅

37

With pearl-drops lingering in their pendent blooms,
Grow golden lilies, red chrysanthemums.
Conceal'd nearby, in sedgy marshland, live
A pair of crickets, spry and talkative.
Arachne from her self-spun endless sleaves
Has clothed in silk the yellow malva leaves.
The tall flowers, as evening claims her own,
Under the wind their lonely heads incline.

38

In the rich house the girls laugh and sing:
The festival Begging Good Luck is in full swing.
At fall of dusk the simple cottager,
Seeing the night approach, makes fast his door.
Our women having Silver Weave in care,
And Heavenly Herd being the men's affair,
No need to pray those river-ferrying stars
With lovers' joys to load our household jars.

39

The orange grub, which time must soon translate,
Like silkworm enters upon its middle state,
Between the boughs, enclosed in a cocoon
Of leaf-like tegument, to dangle down.
And now, shedding the husk, it blossoms forth
Into a brilliant many-colour'd moth,
Whose budded wings, bedew'd with natal spray,
She first unfolds, then stretches out to dry.

40

Here Madam Spider spins and weaves
Her web under the low eaves,
Plotting to take and hold in snare
The wing'd unwary passenger.
A dragonfly and bees, in dire suspense,
Hang there for evidence:
Which sight so little pleases my old age,
I send my rustic boy to raise the siege.

41

Now fields ready for scythe are all our care,
And heavy grows the burden of the year.
Afraid lest winter storms untimely come,
And cold weather deal the harvest doom,
We'll send a letter to the heavenly lord
Praying him not to plunder our small hoard:
For half the crop must go to pay our debts,
The other half in taxes to the state.

42

Autumn come, and *chia tzu* so near,
Mischance of rain is now our only fear.
But happy dawns the day: unclouded time
Enfolds ten thousand doings in one dream.
Harvest gather'd, we take the unthresh'd grain
And spread it in the sun,
Praying the weather may continue good
Until our barns receive the ripen'd food.

43

A clear autumnal night! A full moon!
The solitary scene is all my own.
The moony water stretching wide and bare,
On idle oar I enter the tranced air.
Water and sky, suspending like a dream,
Contain me in a vast besilver'd room.
Who then would live in town,
Where such illumination is unknown?

44

Through the new-built yard, smooth as looking-glass,
Group after group of busy workers pass:
For the threshing of rice-grain they come together,
Taking advantage of fine frosty weather.
Rustic voices, joking, singing, rumbling,
Are like a remote thunder's gentle grumbling;
And all night long, till the first glimmer of dawn,
The rhythmic beat of the flail goes on and on.

45

Until the excisemen open their barn doors
To take of us these tributary stores,
Loaded with pearly grain as white as frost
Our waiting ships must lie along the coast.
Without complaint we render what is due:
Out of two *chung* we do not grudge one *hu*.
For still there's left to us, when all's done,
Some husky rice to feed the children on.

46

Rich store of pulse and corn, this thriving year,
Crams to the brim our jars of earthenware.
By heaven's gift of good fermentable grain
We tread already the royal way of wine,
Though hardly knowing, liquor still so new,
If yet to add our leaflings of bamboo.
And now the Day of Double Brightness comes,
With autumn's festal flowers, chrysanthemums.

47

With onions finely minced, this mess of fish
Makes quite a tolerable dish.
But in my heart I feel the west wind blow,
Luring from watery deeps the four-gill'd *lu*:
A thousand oily snow-white slips are laid
Once more before me, neatly filleted.
O fond pretence! Only in Pine River
Is that immortal fin seen to quiver!

48

Nightlong endures this unexpected frost,
A sign that autumn nears her end at last:
The woods, where yesterday only greenness was,
Wear now a richly-embroidered silken dress.
Here, in my orange-garden's secret air,
Another transformation is astir:
Hidden among these leaves of emerald
Ten thousand golden spheres are safe in fold.

Winter

斜日低山片月高

49

Low lie the hills as day goes slowly down:
High above is a pale slice of moon.
Drowsy from sleep I swallow my due potion,
Then take a stroll to set my blood in motion.
Tall trees, assaulted by the frosty wind,
With twice ten thousand leaves scatter the ground.
Leaning upon my staff, I noddingly
Compute how many herons' nests there be.

50

Like a man at his own hearth this elderly one
Under the eaves he stands, his back to the sun.
Warmth like wine, a glowing gradual bliss,
Blurs his sense with heavenly drowsiness.
Suddenly a horse goes galloping past the gate:
What man is the rider, and what his office of state,
Who, hat askew, clutching his reins, whipping his horse,
In face of the bleak north wind follows a struggling course?

51

Now add we to the roof another patch
Of dried rushes to reinforce the thatch;
Like monks' pavilions safe from winter's harm,
With thicker clay-cast make our houses warm.
So we be safe inside, and he without,
Let the wind roar at his pleasure and tear about,
While we within enjoy the music he makes,
Playing his flute in the fence of bamboo-stakes.

52

A pine-tree flare instead of a candle-cage
Befits my rusticating age:
Like black ink the aroma drifting slow
Hangs in the air of room and portico.
When evening comes I approach the dark pane
Of the south window and wipe its paper clean:
The which no sooner done
Than instantly it fills with reddening sun.

53

Here, where the crust of the world cracks,
Under the constellation of the Ox
We raise to the earth-spirit our simple shrine,
Ritually offering leg of pork, and wine.
When bulls and cows from pestilence are free,
Calves wax fat and flourish stalwartly.
Next year we plan to extend our farm ground
Eastward, beyond the city's bound.

54

Let the boat take me leisurely where it will,
So of these snow-bright slopes I have my fill.
The wind falls, is still. Cold and fine,
The evening air grows ever more crystalline.
The rhythmic pole makes music in my ears
Like breaking jade or shatter of pearly spheres:
By which I guess the water's shining face
Already wears a brittle sheet of ice.

55

Sweeping away the snow, we gather now
Cabbages of the sort called 'spreading low':
Like honey'd lotus-roots are they, for scent,
And in the mouth even more succulent.
At the grand house with the red-painted gate,
Where for unfastidious palates there's much to eat,
There they regard this heavenly vegetable
As merely another dish, and undelectable.

56

Throughout the long, unending night of snow,
His knobs of smokeless charcoal burn and glow.
On earthen hearth he warms the wine, whose steam,
As night wears on, with fragrance fills the room.
'Don't blame old wife,' she says, 'for lack of care,
Because no dish of food she did prepare!'
And shows him, smiling, where, for his comfort's sake,
Taroes and chestnuts in the ashes bake.

57

Between the feast of La and first of spring
There's wine to make ready and set a-simmering,
So by good luck we'll never lack to hear
The clink of brimming greentops all the year.
You who live in the towns with noise and smoke,
How are you better off than country folk,
Especially now, when new rules ordain
We send you not our luscious millet-grain?

58

A yellow tax-paper brings good luck your way.
Not so the white: that means you have to pay.
A smooth black-coated gentleman from town
Arrives one day at noon:
'How tiresome the caprices of the great!
My honour'd seniors, ministers of state
Whose ordinance one cannot but comply with,
Beg your green-insect money to buy wine with.'

59

A well-born youth, in quest of blossoming plum,
To the faggot-door of my small cottage is come.
North and south the barren branches sway,
Still unaware that spring is on the way.
All of a sudden, turning his lordly head,
He sees a flowering peach-tree, damask red.
Celestial sight! It sets him wondering
Am I perhaps a native of Wu Ling?

[34]

60

In village highways, when the year ends,
Each winter sees a festival of friends.
Good neighbours won't neglect, for anything,
The ritual of the mutual visiting.
In long, linen garments, white as snow,
From house to wooden house the old men go.
'Give you good den,' they'll say. ''Twas made at home,
This gown of mine: wove on our own loom.'

NOTES

BY TSUI CHI

❀

Poem 3

The Festival of Purity and Brightness is a festival inspiring to
poets. According to the old lunar calendar, it was either the
fifth or the sixth day of the fourth moon, and thus it indicates
the end of the spring season. This engenders in the people a
sentiment of farewell to the best season of the year. For the
Chinese summer is hot and unpleasant. The festival is cele-
brated by a ceremonial of picnicking outside the cities. People
sojourn in the countryside with their families and friends. It
is called 'The Tramping on the Green'. Family sepulchres
are visited, and the dust wiped from the tombs, on which new
earth is piled. Sacrifices are offered to the ancestral spirits.
The day, as it appears in poetry, is often wet, with almond
flowers blossoming and willow trees teeming with life in the
rain.

Poem 4

'Faggots and Rushes' is also the name of a cheap wine.
(*Chiu Shih.*)

Poem 4

The country inn is literally in Chinese 'a flag pavilion'. It is
an officially managed house, selling wine:

The wine-flag towers from the willow trees, wafting in the breeze,
A thatched house stands at the foot of the sloping hill.

—as a poet sees it, this is a general picture of the ancient
country inn.

[36]

Poem 5

It is an ancient Chinese custom to put money in the coffins of the dead, so that the ghosts may not be in want. As silk was at times used as currency, this was sometimes buried too. About the fifth century, the Marquis Tung-hun of Ch'i used paper money instead of silk. The burning of the paper money at the graveside is a token of its being given to the dead.

Poem 7

'Salad Festival' of the 'Cold Meal' day occurs 106 days after the Winter Solstice. The legend runs that when the young Prince Chung-erh of Tsin was in exile, his loyal friends followed him abroad through difficult years. The prince returned to his own country and became the powerful duke, the Civilized. He rewarded all his friends except one Chieh T'ui, the greatest friend of all. Without complaining, Chieh T'ui escaped to the mountains, away from the knowledge of society, and lived as a hermit. Later, when the duke came to remember him and became ashamed of his own ingratitude, he searched the mountain, and endeavoured to scorch the obstinate hermit out of his shelter. But Chieh T'ui had now made up his mind to refuse any reward, and as the flames spread, he remained where he was and was burnt to death. This tragic end so saddened the hearts of the gods, that they loathed the sight of fire from that day. In the district of Tsin a custom later developed that no fires must be built on that day. The oven and hearth in the kitchen must remain cold, and only salad must be eaten. In poetry it often appears to be a rainy day, a haze covering the willow trees on the river banks.

Poem 7

Ling Yen, the 'Divine Cliff', is to the west of Soochow. There are on the cliffs the remains of the palaces of the beautiful Queen Hsi Shih, one of which was her 'Terrace of the Lute'.

Hu Ch'iu, the 'Tiger's Slope', is sometimes called Hai Yung

Shan—'The Hill of the Rising Sea'. Standing to the north-west of the city of Soochow, it is famous for its beauty. Three days after the burial of an ancient prince at the spot, according to the legends, a white tiger appeared and squatted on the top of his sepulchre. Hence the derivation of the name Tiger's Slope.

Poem 13

Heng Tang is a famous lake, south-west of Soochow. To the north was the Maple Bridge, and to the south the Lake of Dimple. On the shores was a town called Heng Tang, the girls of which town are famous for their beauty.

Poem 14

The season of the 'Yellowing Plum' is marked by rainy weather. This period occurs about the end of the fourth moon of the year in the Soochow district, and when moisture is plentiful in the air the mellowing plum fruits turn gold-coloured and fall.

Poem 16

Shang Ch'ih was the first '*ch'ih*' day in the first decade of the third moon (cf. Poem 42, Note). On this day people went to bathe in eastward-flowing streams in order to get rid of any ill luck, which was then carried away to the eastern seas by the flowing water. The day was later on fixed as the third of the month.

Poem 23

This fish is sometimes called the 'stone-headed' because of the hard bone which is in its head. Its scientific name is perhaps *Sciaena schlegeli*.

Poem 32

It was the ancient tradition to plant three elm trees outside the emperor's court. These marked the position facing which three of the emperor's ministers, with the equivalent rank of 'duke', stood. Hence the 'three trees' symbolized high rank in the court.

Poem 36

'The art of being dull of sense' is to play foolish and deaf, when required; there is a Chinese saying:

> *Unless you are foolish and deaf,*
> *You cannot become a good parent-in-law.*

A story is told of a haunted house wherein dwelt a fierce demon, which transformed itself into horrible beings in order to frighten its victim to death. Sometimes, however, it changed into a beautiful woman, and hurt the man who fell in love with 'her'. An old monk, blind and deaf, happened to lodge in the same house and sat up all night alone, meditating. The demon came and tried to tempt or frighten him, but with no success. The monk could neither hear nor see, and was quite ignorant of its existence. The demon sighed and withdrew, and, perhaps ashamed of itself, vanished for ever.

Poem 38

The granddaughter of the Emperor of the Heavens was in love with the Herd of the Sky. This love affair provoked the Emperor to fury, and he decided that the young couple must be separated by the Silver River (the Milky Way), across which they could see one another, but could not hear one another speak, nor could they meet. At her stern grandfather's order, the young princess was told to weave a damask which could never be woven. This was the rainbow-like tatters of cloud which appear in the golden dusk. The princess's love-sickness therefore never ceased. But after a long time her royal grandfather began to pity her, and allowed her to meet the Herd on the other side of the River once a year on the seventh day of the seventh moon. On that evening the Divine Magpies would fly in a chain over the river and make a bridge for the girl to cross. The next day the white magpies disappeared from the sky, and we find the Weaving Girl back at her work beyond the reach of the Herd.

This is only a story of the stars, but down in our mundane world this is the Love Festival, which is called 'The Night of Begging Good Luck' (*ch'iao hsi*), or—because *chi* (begging) can also mean seven—'The Night of Seven Good Lucks'. In the noontime Chinese girls and women play a game of divination: they put coloured silk through the 'seven holes' of a specially made needle and throw this on a bowl of water placed in the sun. 'The needle stays afloat' and the lady looks at the shadow to see the omen, which appears in various forms —clouds, flowers, animals, shoes, scissors, etc. These pictures determine the future of the questioner's love affair.

Poem 39

When the poet mentions the transforming orange grub, he probably alludes to the philosophy of the existence of human beings. How transient and unreal is life! One can find noble pleasure in an orange as much as in society and the court. The book *Yu Kuai Lu* describes the story of the 'old men in the orange' of the Pa-Ch'iung orchard. There grew on one tree a large orange like an earthen jar. Somebody cut it open and found, seated inside, two old men playing chess. They told their discoverer that in the orange it was as pleasant as on the hermit's hills of Shang Shan. One thing they regretted about their orange abode was that whilst the hermit's hill was deeprooted in the earth, the world inside the orange was so unstable that it could be removed from its stalk at any time.

Poem 42

The Chinese counted the days in the month by a combined system of two branches of starry names, one containing ten names beginning with the word *chia*, and the other twelve names beginning with *tzu*. When interpolated, these compose sixty different names. *Chia-tzu* is the first day of a unit-cycle.

Poem 43

The Chinese used a lunar calendar, and the night of the fifteenth of the eighth moon, when the moon becomes full, is called the Middle Autumn Festival. The ancient queen Ch'ang O, wife of the Great Archer, according to legend, was entrusted by her husband with the care of some elixir, the eater of which would become immortalized. The queen swallowed the medicine herself, and acquired the art of flying into the air. But her husband chased after her, and she fled to the Heavenly World and became the Goddess of the Moon. This new rank did not bring her much pleasure, for looking down at the noisy world, where romances occur endlessly, she became lovesick and lonely:

Ch'ang O must regret that she has swallowed the elixir:
Night after night the sea is blue, the sky emerald, and her lonely heart is never consoled.

So sings the poet Li Shang-yin.

Poem 46

The Festival of Double Brightness is, by the Chinese calendar, the ninth day of the ninth moon—the number nine is a masculine number and the symbol of 'brightness', while number six is 'shadowy' and feminine. The chrysanthemum is in full bloom at this season, and it is the custom to admire this flower with a feast of wine and crabs. The poet Tao Ch'ien was a great lover of this flower, and the festival also preserves the poet's memory. According to the book *Hsu Ch'i Hsieh Chi*, a gentleman named Huan was the friend of a magician, who warned him that calamity of the epidemic kind would spread and ruin the town, but if Huan would go with his family to some mountain on the ninth day of the ninth moon, each wearing a bag of stuffed *chu yu* grass, and drink wine spiced with chrysanthemum petals, their lives could be saved. This they did, and when they returned home in the evening, they found the dead bodies of chickens, dogs and sheep strewn on the ground. A custom was developed on the strength of this legend. On that day of every year people would climb up mountains, wearing the *chu yu* grass. Each member of the family was given a spike of grass, and anyone absent from the gathering would be remembered by the rest of the family. Abroad, the traveller would feel homesick on this day, as the poet says:

> *In my mind's eye, I see my brothers climbing the mountains;*
> *While they distribute the* chu yu *flowers, they find one of their*
> *beloved ones absent.*

Poem 47

The *lu* fish is a Chinese perch. Usually it has two gills, but the fish living in the Pine River, west of a town of that name to the east of Soochow, has four and is particularly delicious. The poet Su Shih admires it in his famous poem 'The Red Cliff'. The fish is best cooked with a green vegetable called *hsun ts'ai*. In the third century a poet, Chang Han, from Soochow travelled to the north, and served in the court of the prince Ch'i. But Chang Han soon grew weary of politics, in which he had become involved, and he felt very homesick when the golden wind of autumn blew. He was suddenly seized with a longing desire to have a dinner in his home town, of the *hsun ts'ai* with the four-gilled perch. 'Oh, one should live to please oneself. What is the use of wealth and power which do not please me?' he sighed, and on that same day he resigned his post and drove home in a light chariot. A few months after he had gone, the prince's influence collapsed and he was assassinated. The poet is praised not only for his noble taste, but also for his political foresight. '*Hsun ts'ai* and four-gilled perch' is in the Chinese dictionary a rhetorical term expressing a homesick feeling.

Poem 57

Greentops, literally: 'green at the top of the wine-jar'. The reference is to newly made wine which is yet mellow enough for drinking. An alternative phrase, used by a T'ang poet, was 'Spring at the top of the wine-jar'.

Poem 58

Owing to the metallic alloys in it, Chinese coin looked green, and was known as the 'green coin'. The greenness, however, is also associated with the legend of an insect called the green *fu*. The parental instinct of this insect is so strong that pro-fiteers made use of it. Some mother-insects were killed and their blood smeared on eighty-one (a magic number) coins, also some children-insects were killed and their blood smeared on another eighty-one coins; these were henceforth called mother-money and children-money. These were put together in a jar, and buried 'at the foot of the eastern wall' for three days, until the affection grew to such an extent that they were inseparable from one another. Either the mother-money was used to keep the children-money in safety, or the reverse. In both cases the money paid out would come back to the user voluntarily.

Poem 59

A native of Wu Ling. Once during the Tai Yuan period of the Tsin dynasty, writes the poet Tao Chi'en, a certain fisherman from Wu Ling lost his way and came to a stream. Along the banks of the stream grew innumerable peach trees which were in full bloom. Attracted by their beauty, the fisherman pursued his way among the flowers, and came to a small crack in the mountain. He crept in. The path was extremely narrow at first, then it opened out and the fisherman found himself standing before a populated valley. The residents looked very gay and very kind. All of them seemed to work in the fields, and all were well-to-do. They invited the fisherman to their homes, and entertained him with rice and chicken. They told him that their ancestors had moved into this valley during the disturbing years at the end of the Ch'in dynasty, nearly six centuries ago, and they had never known the political up-heavals which had taken place outside. They were contented and happy, and made the fisherman promise never to reveal their existence to the world. But the fisherman could not keep his word: when he returned from the valley he went to tell the mayor, who instantly sent men in search of the place. Fortunately, the fisherman had lost his own tracks; the mayor died soon after; and the secret remained undiscovered.

www.ingramcontent.com/pod-product-compliance
Ingram Content Group UK Ltd.
Pitfield, Milton Keynes, MK11 3LW, UK
UKHW042149280225
455719UK00001B/214